Traveling In Japan
By Coloring

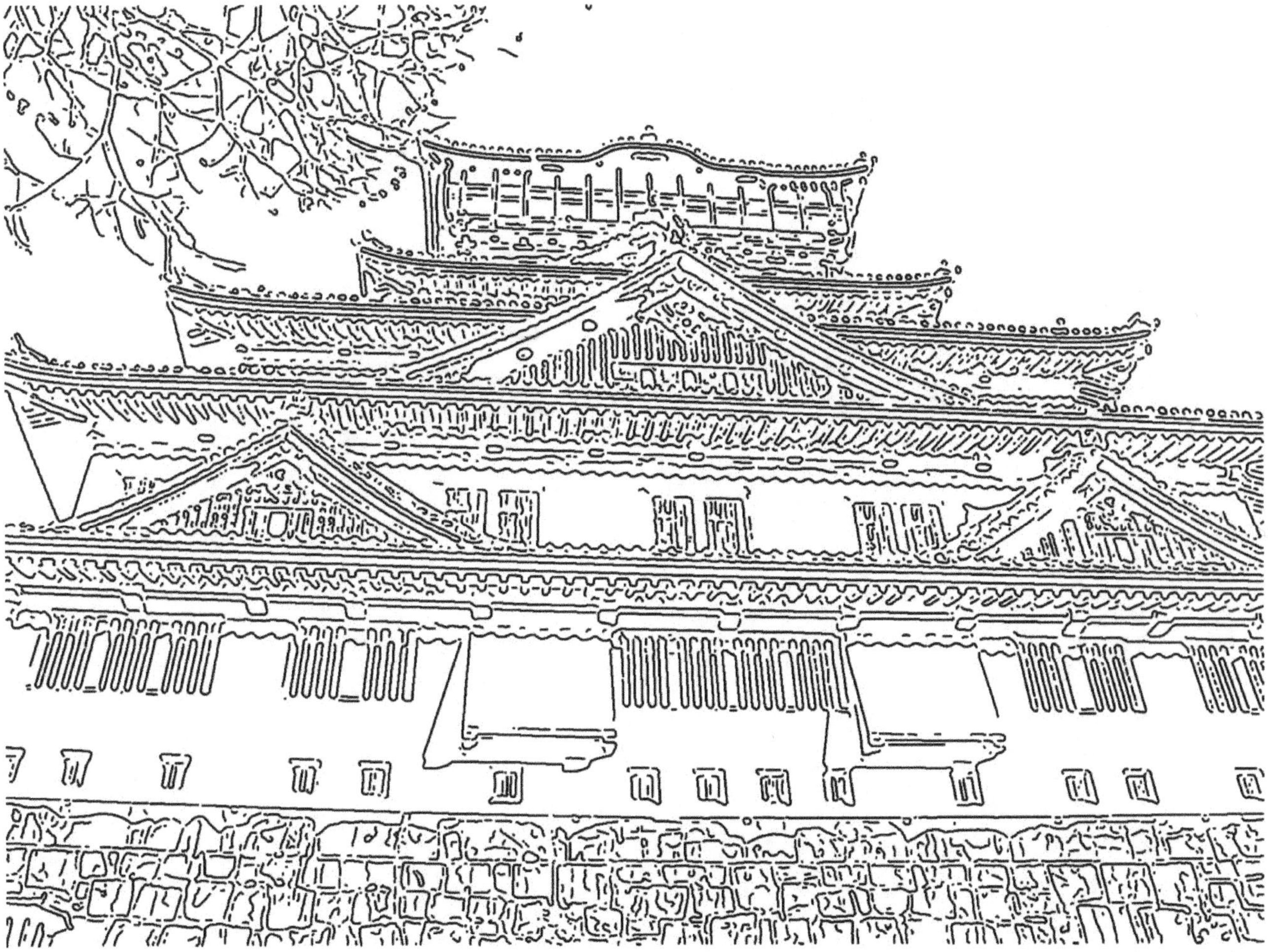

William B. Lewis

T

Mandala : Traveling In Japan By Coloring

Copyright: Published in the United States by William B. Lewis
Published June 2016

ISBN-13: 978-1534779273

ISBN-10: 1534779272

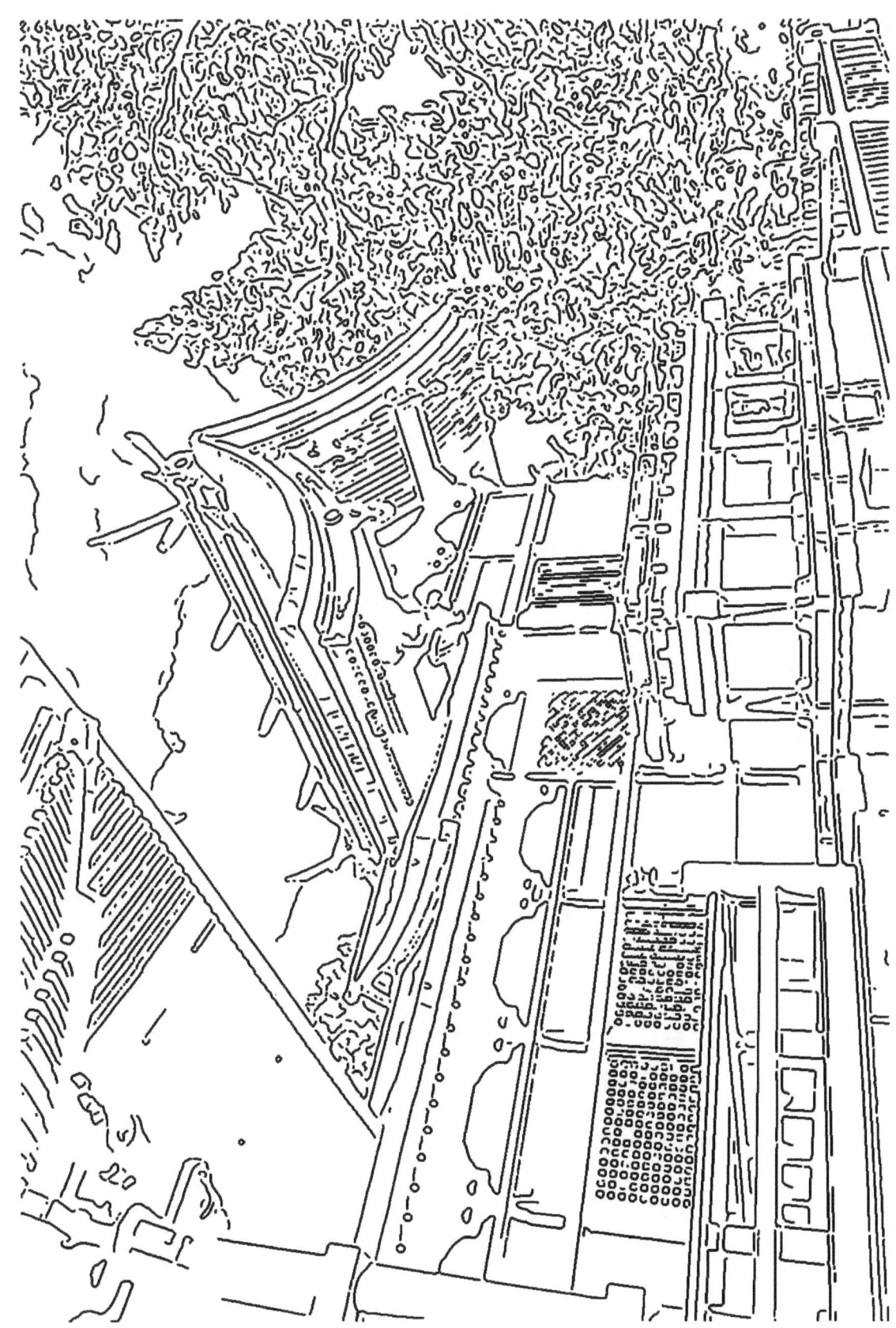

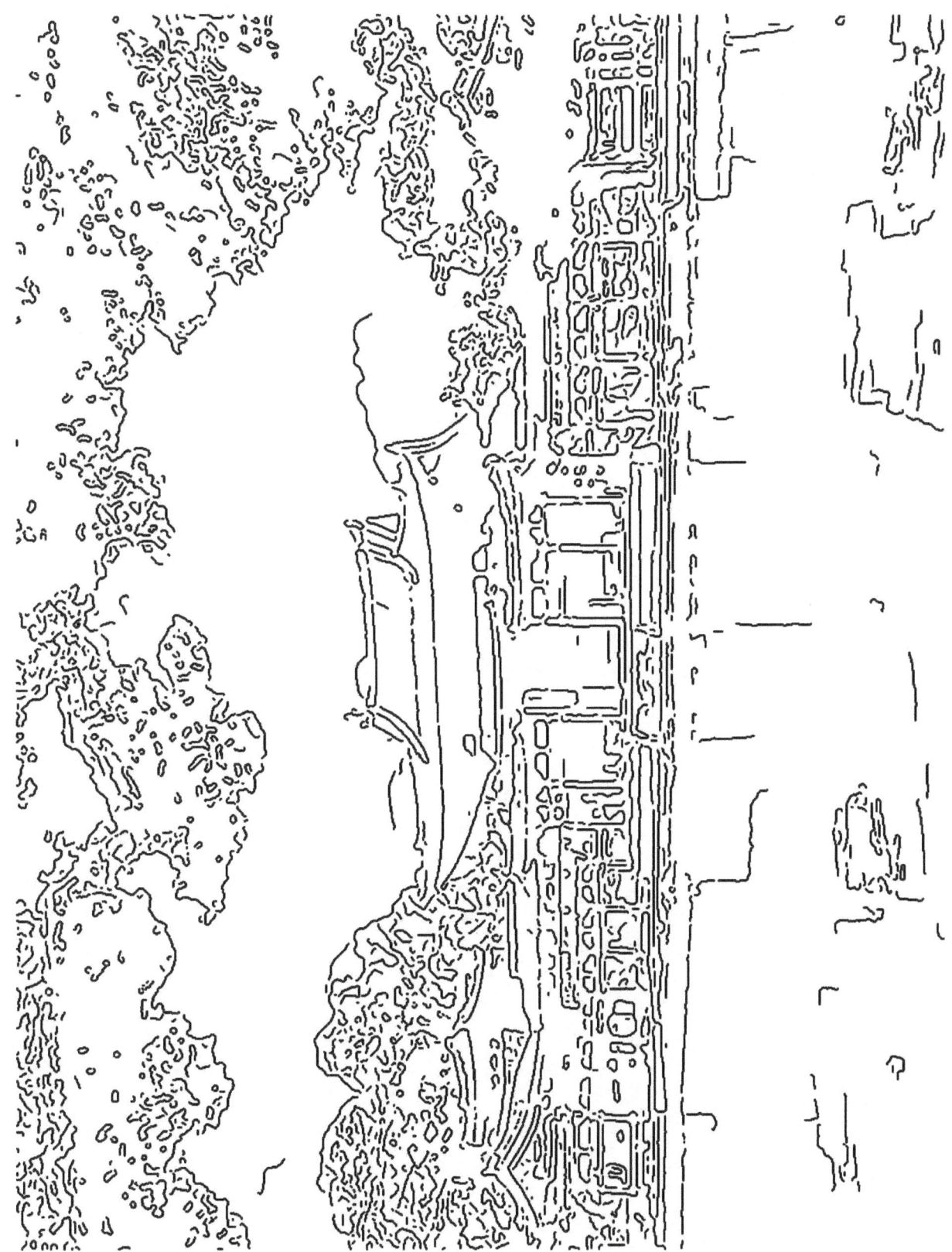

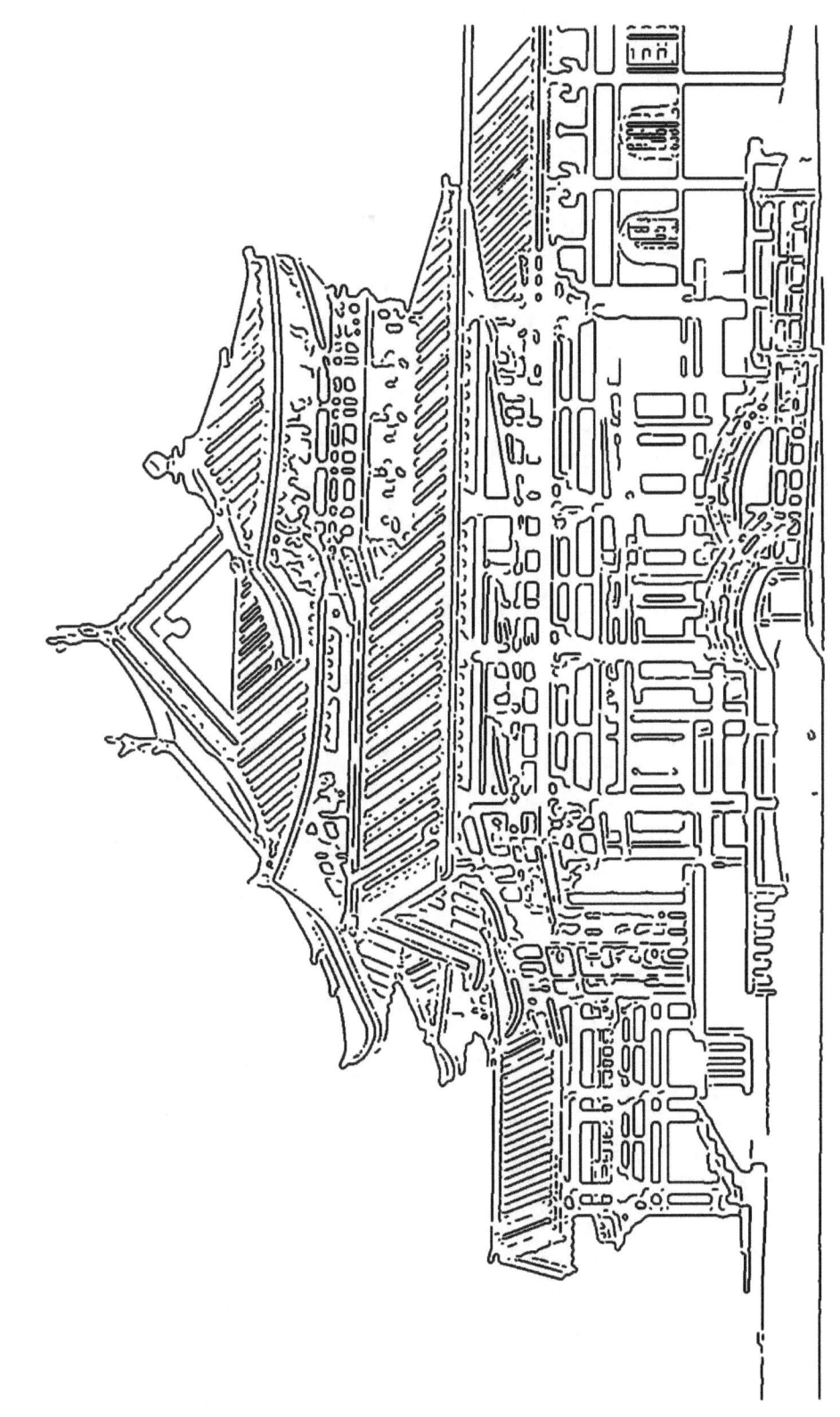

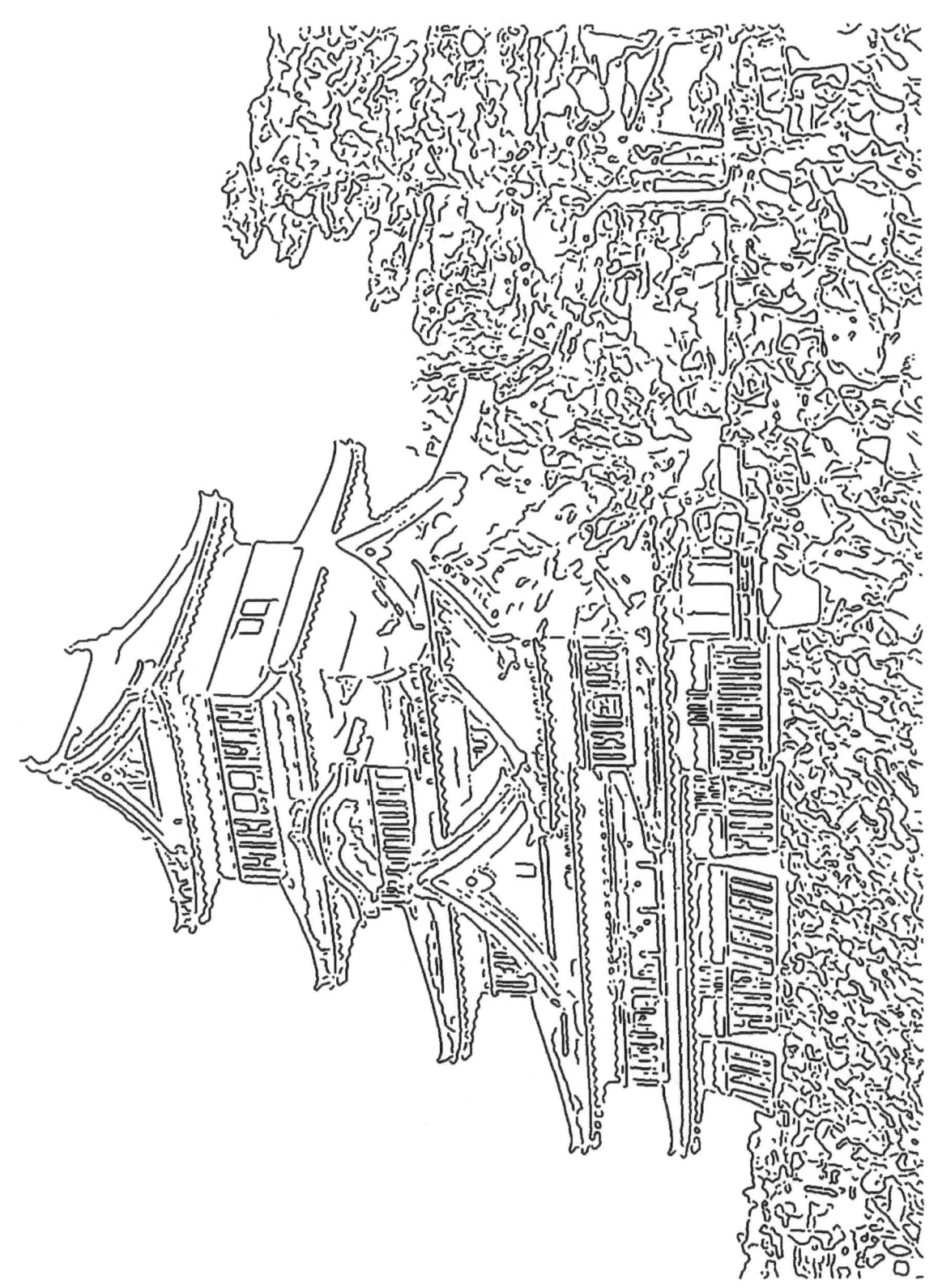

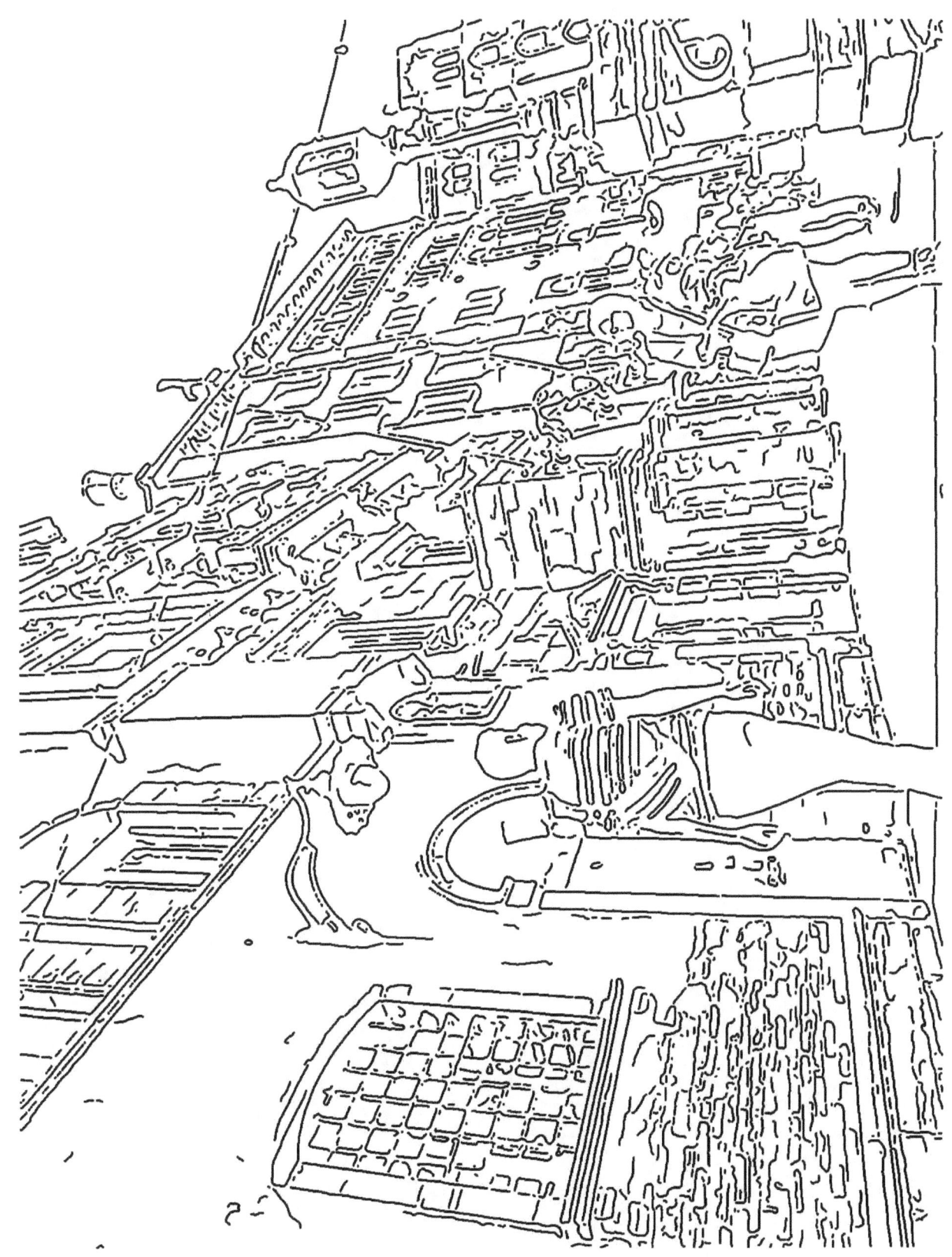

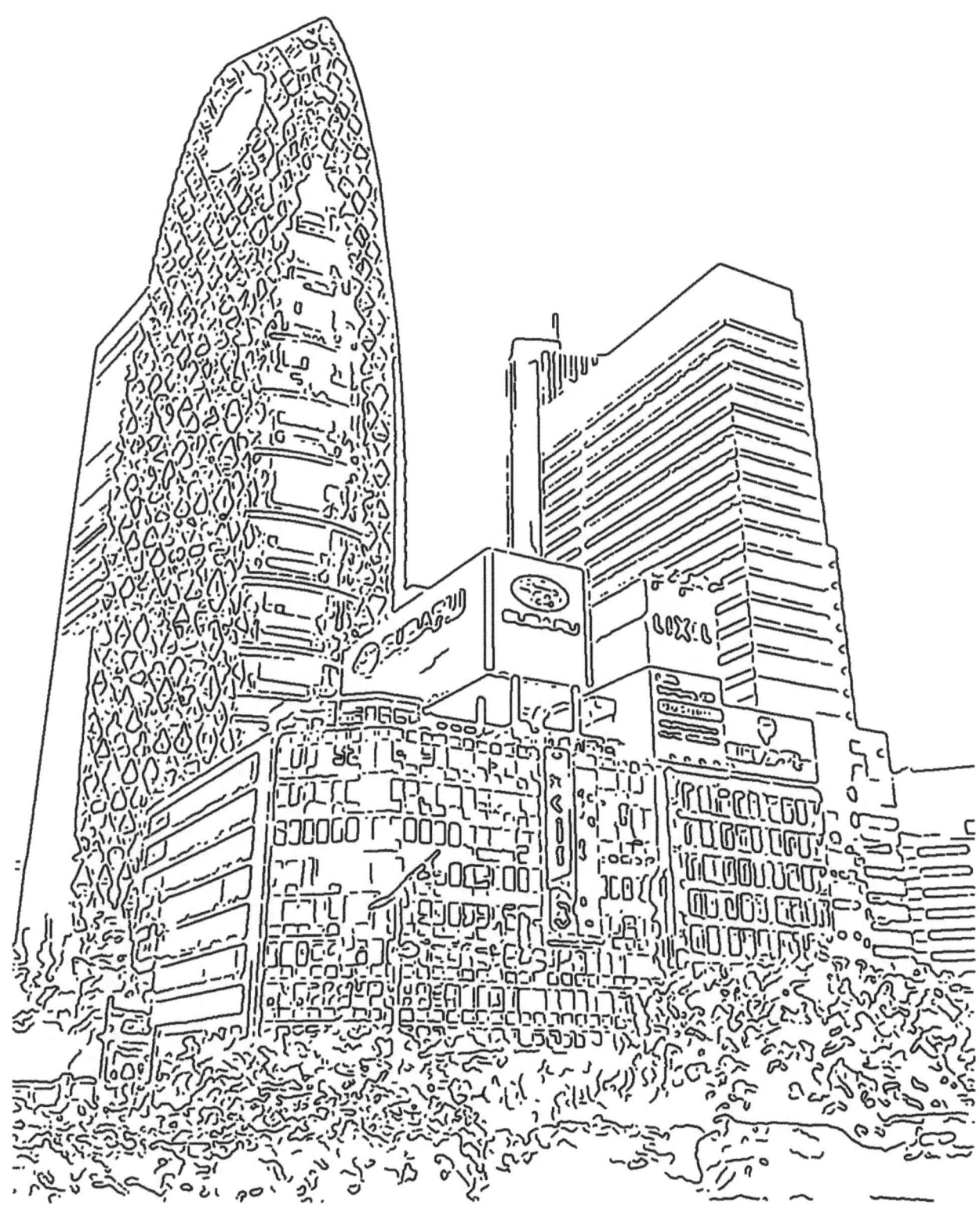

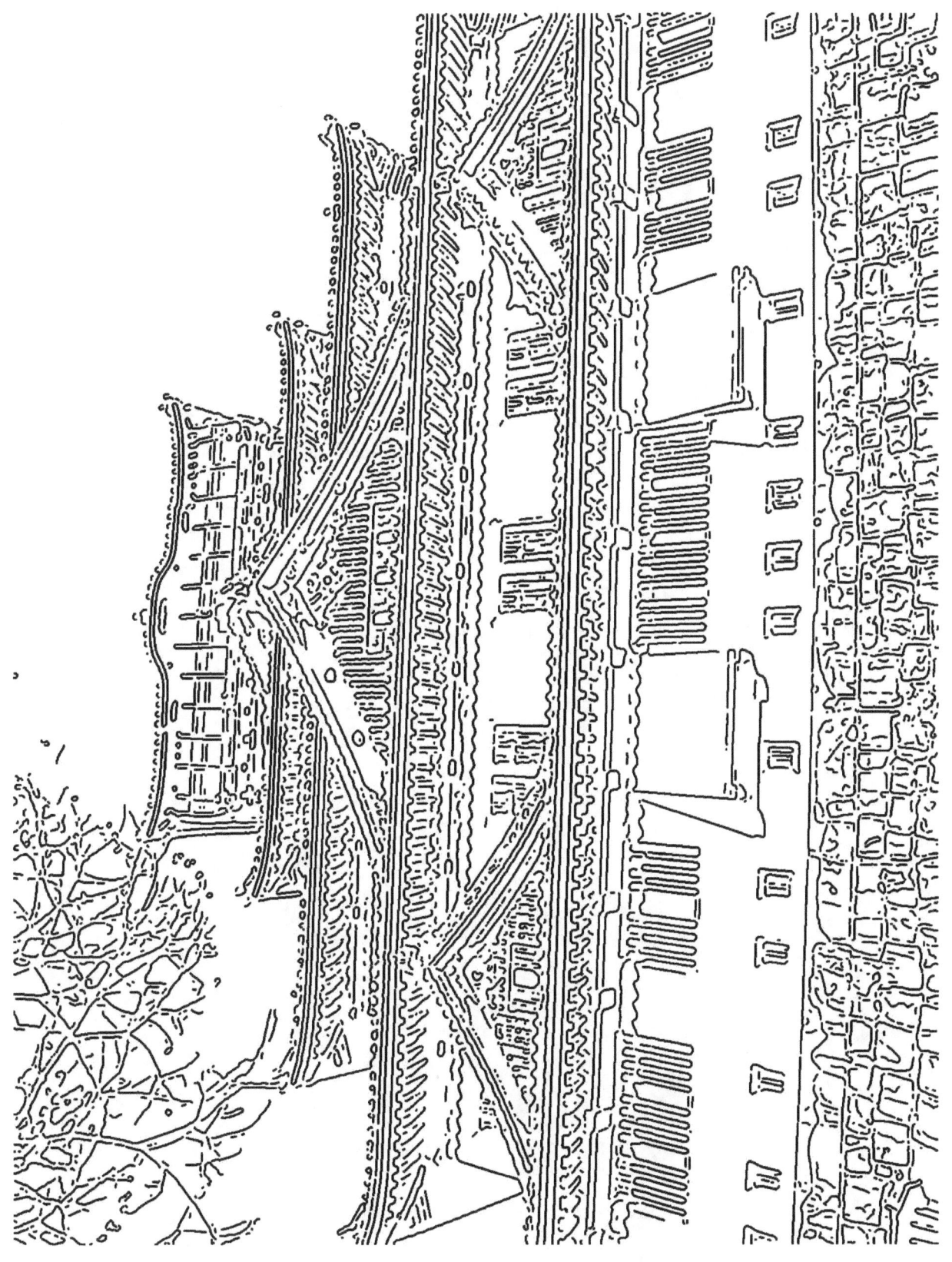

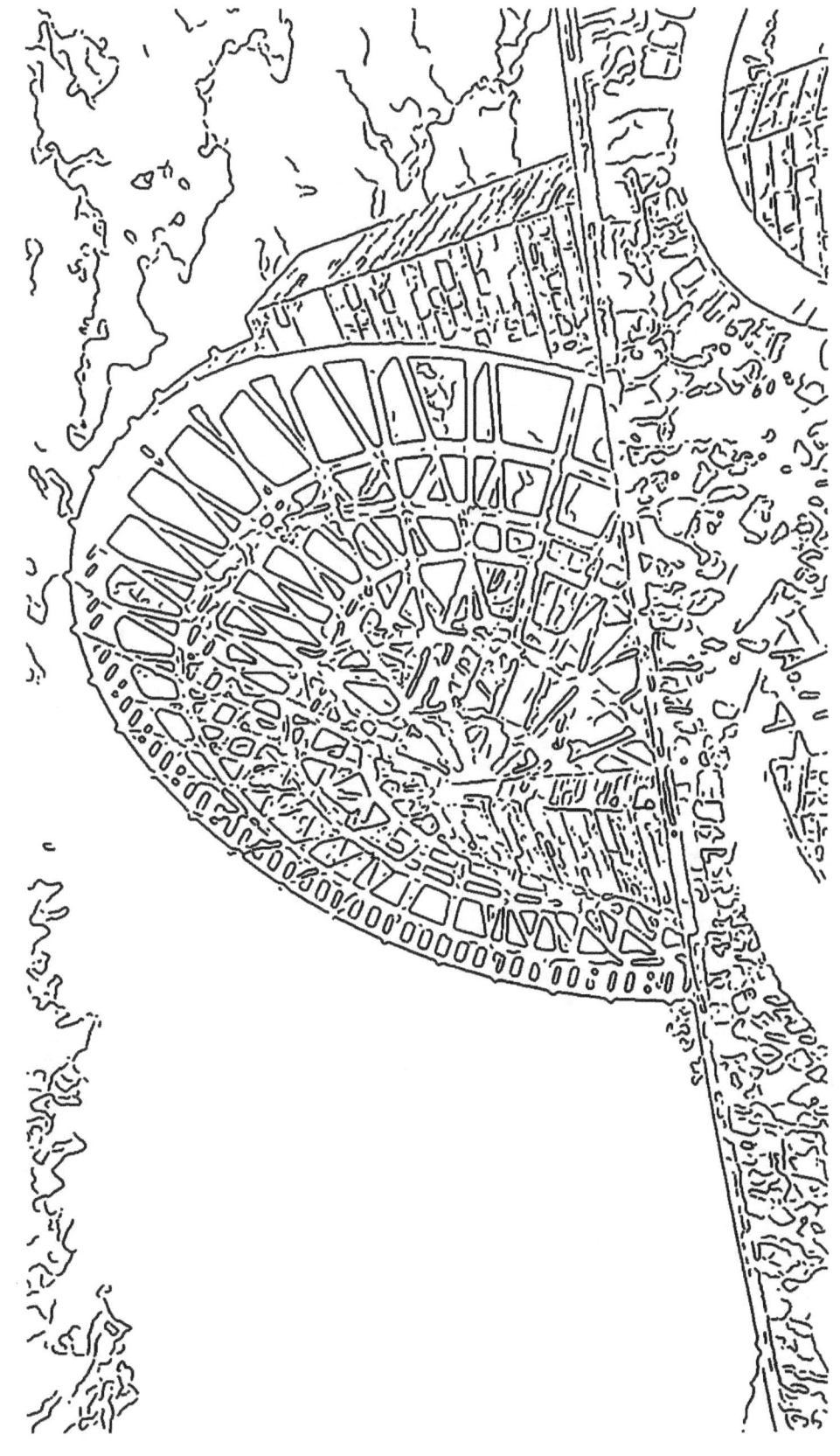

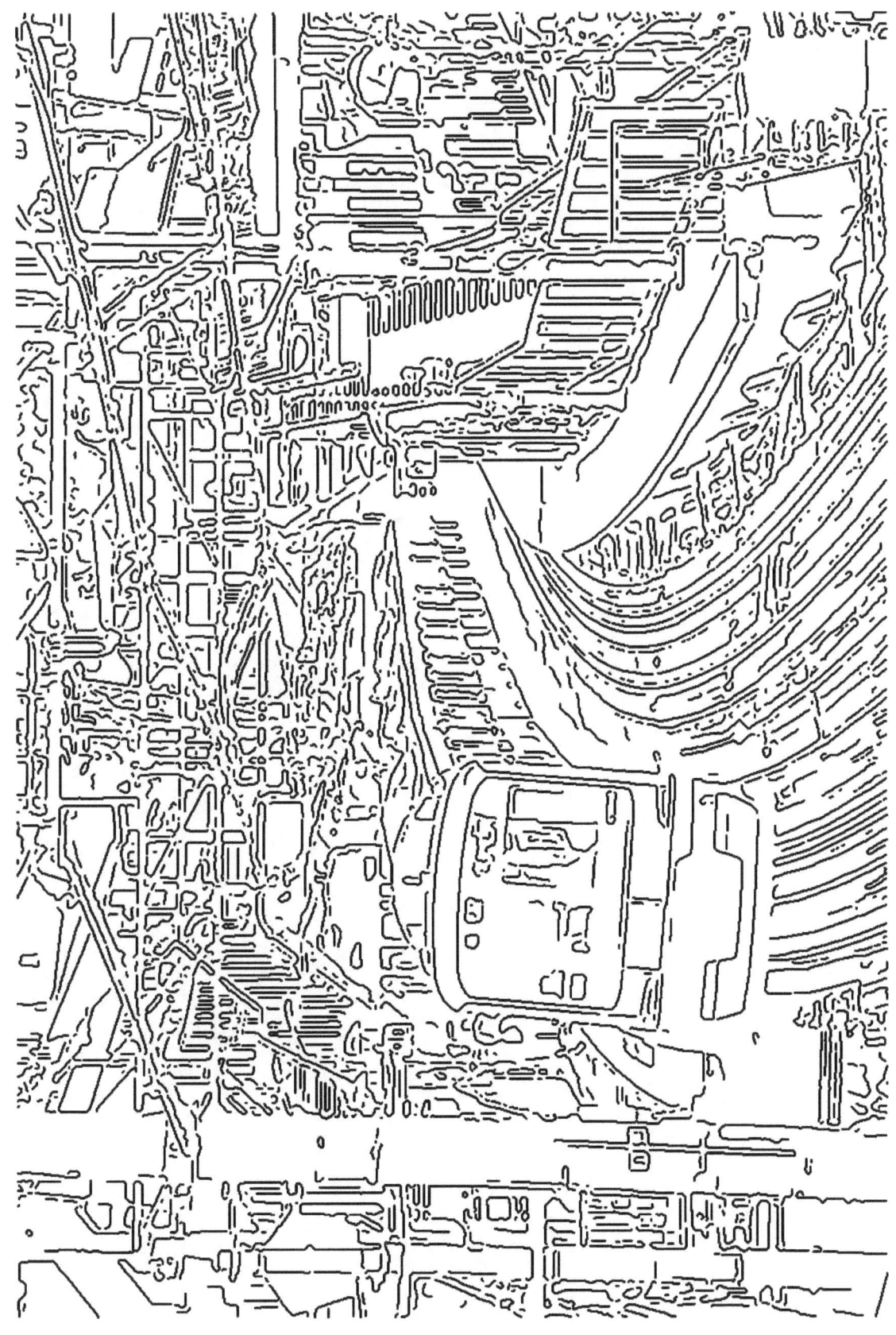

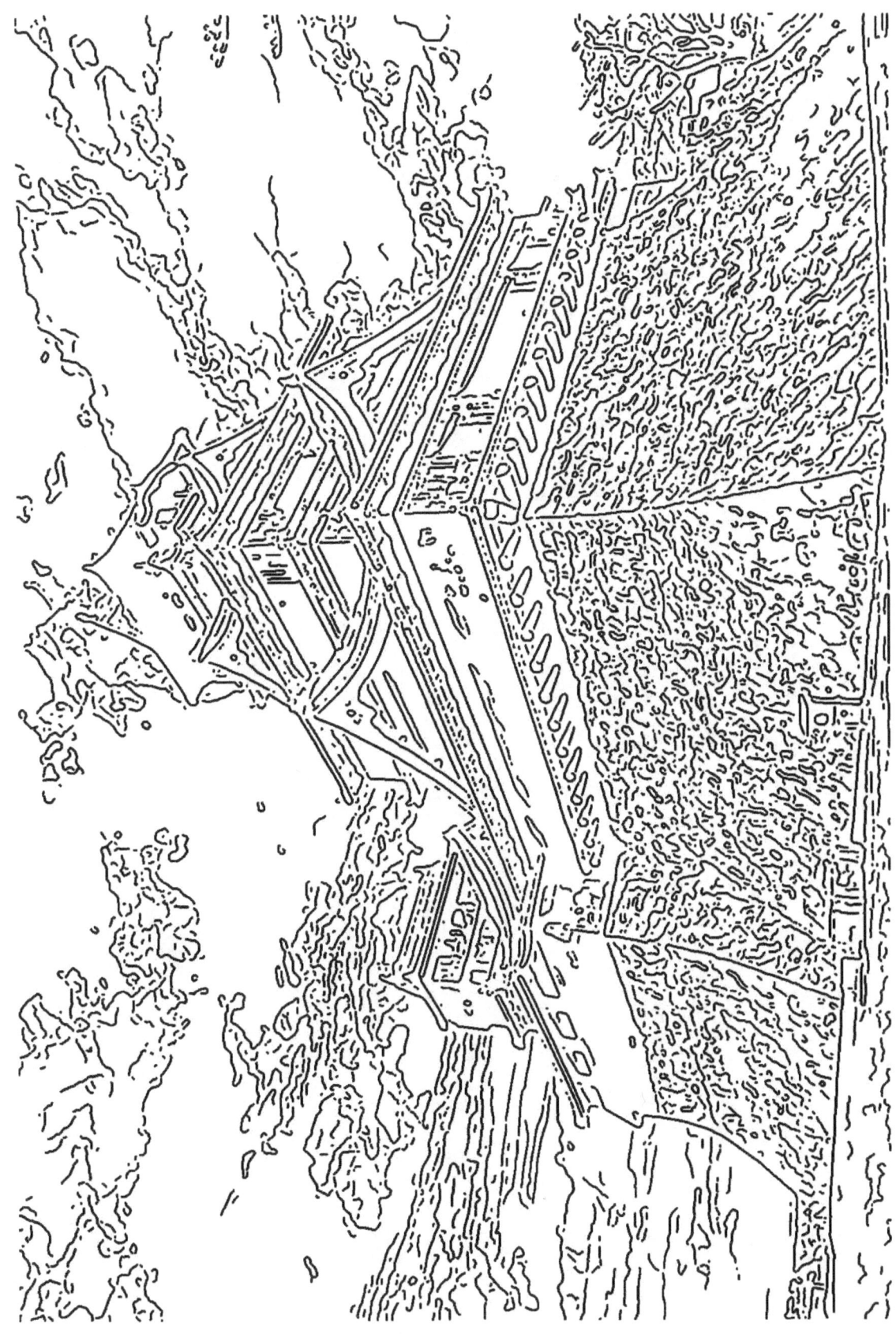

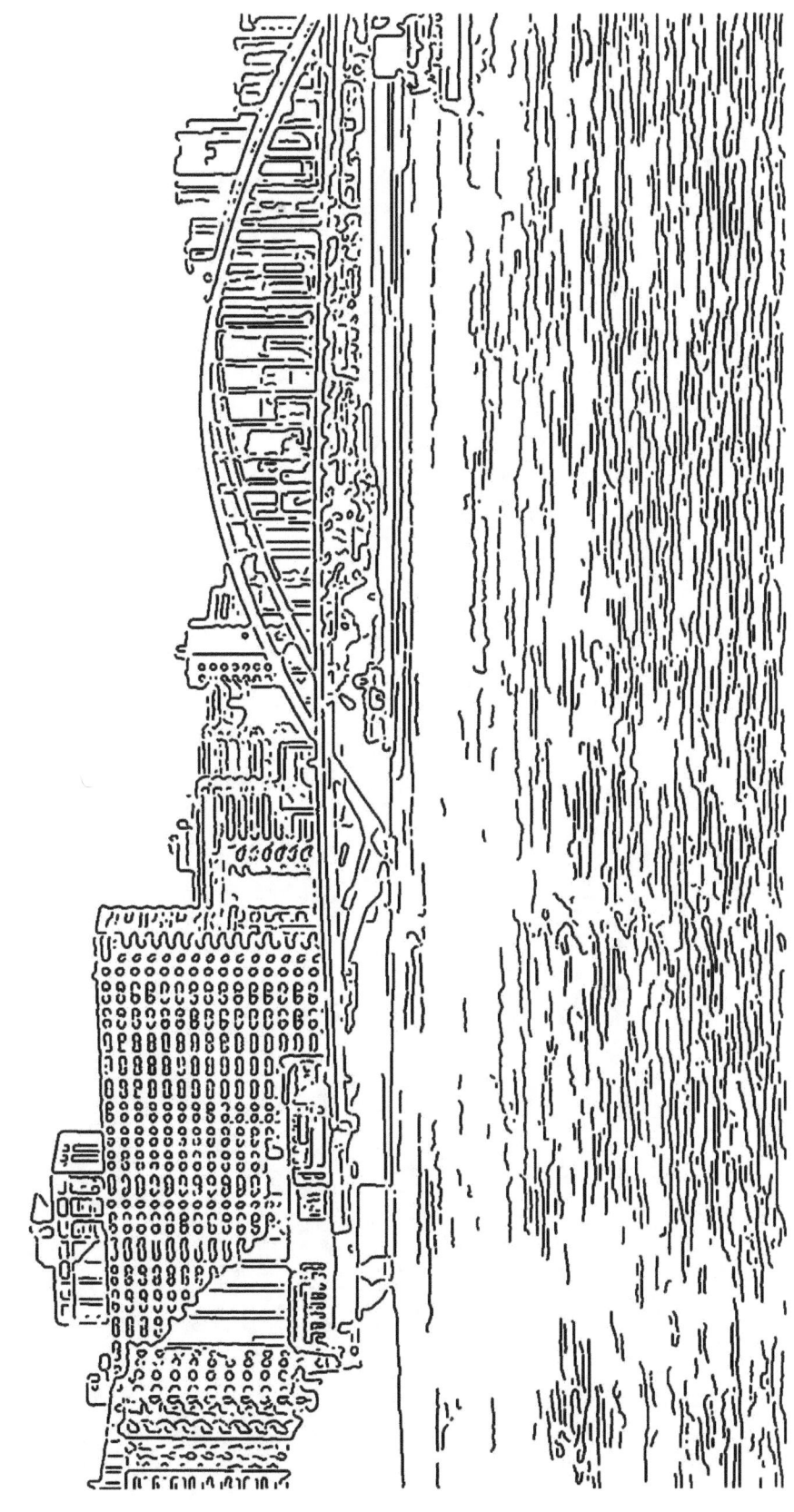

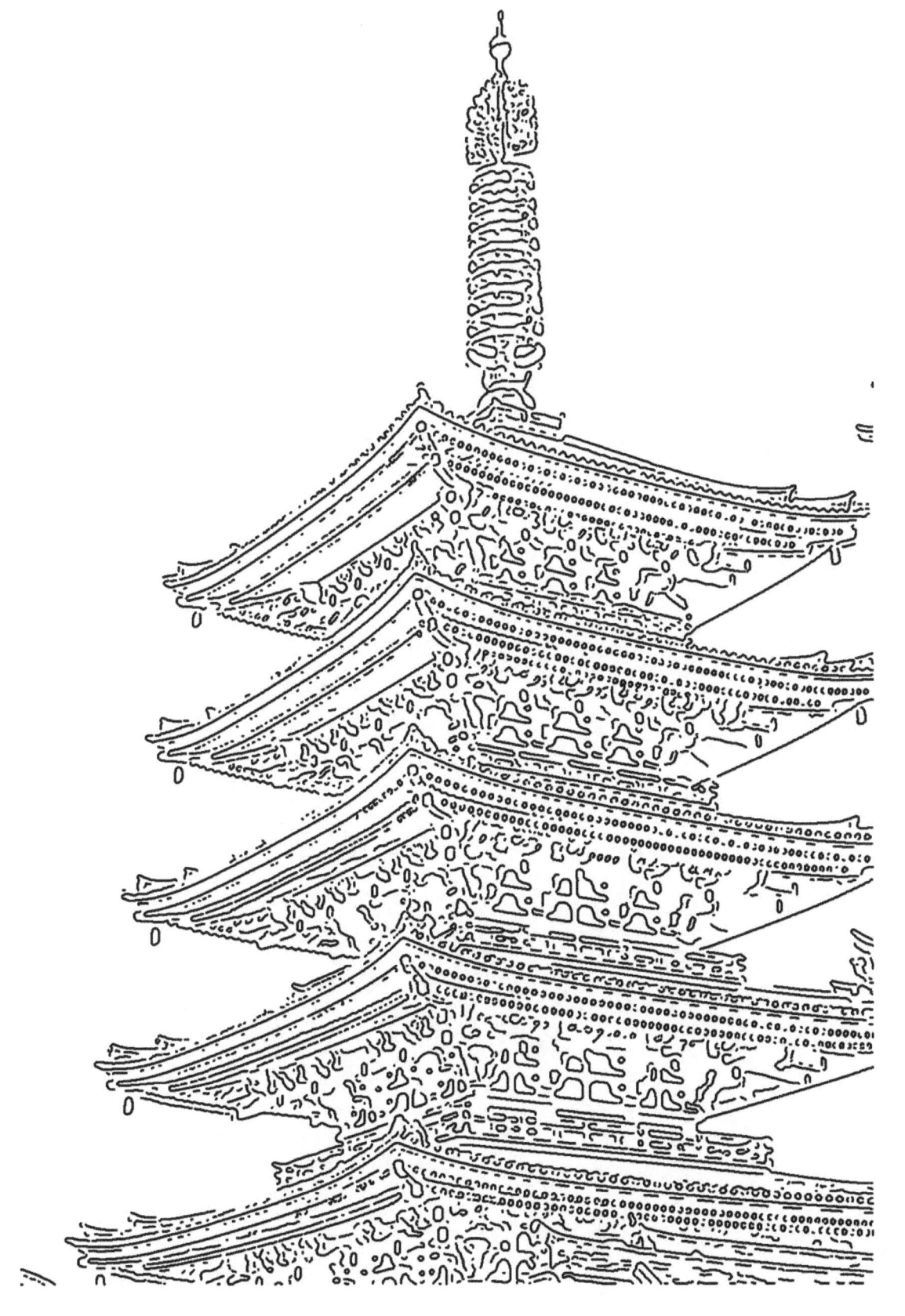

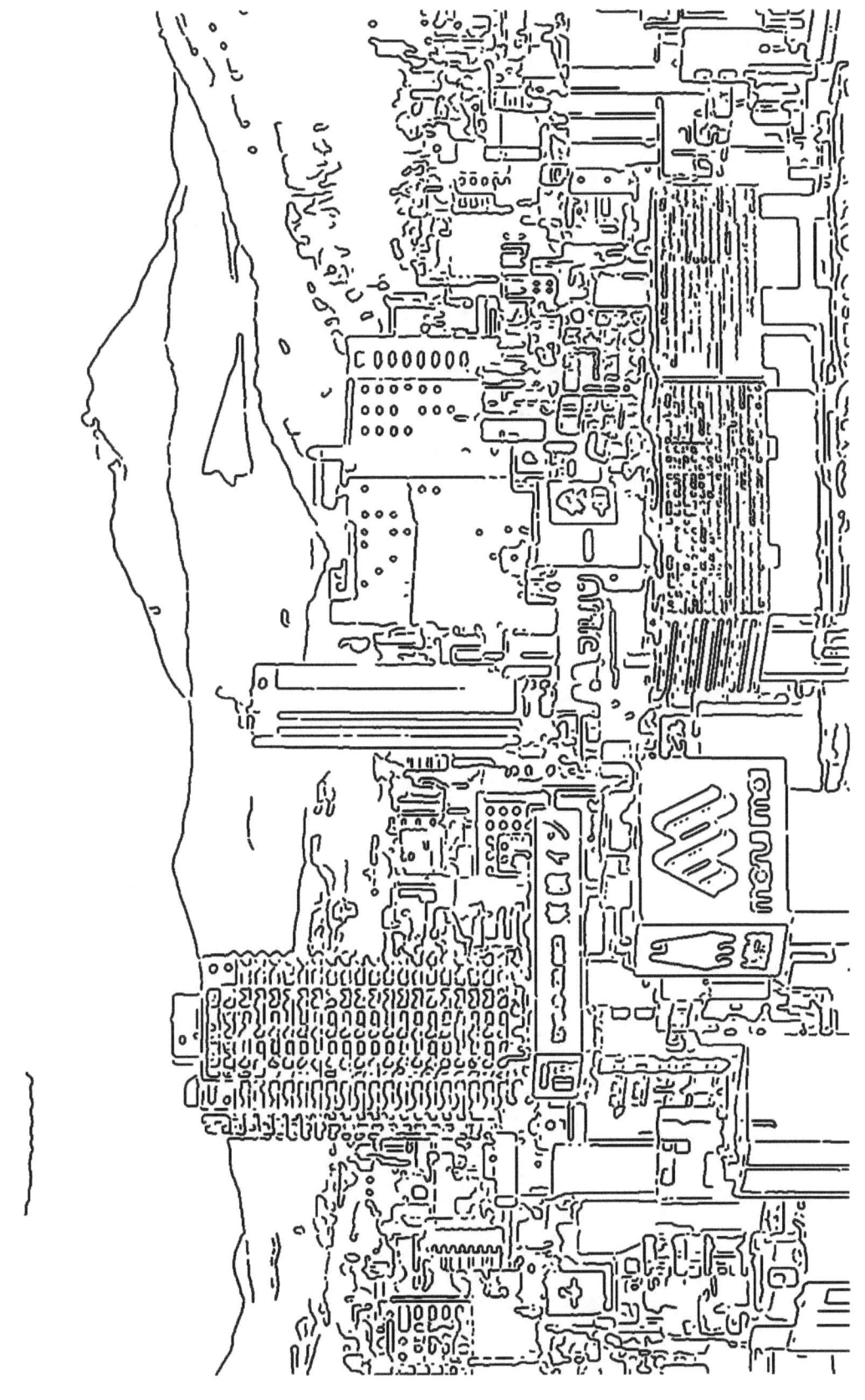

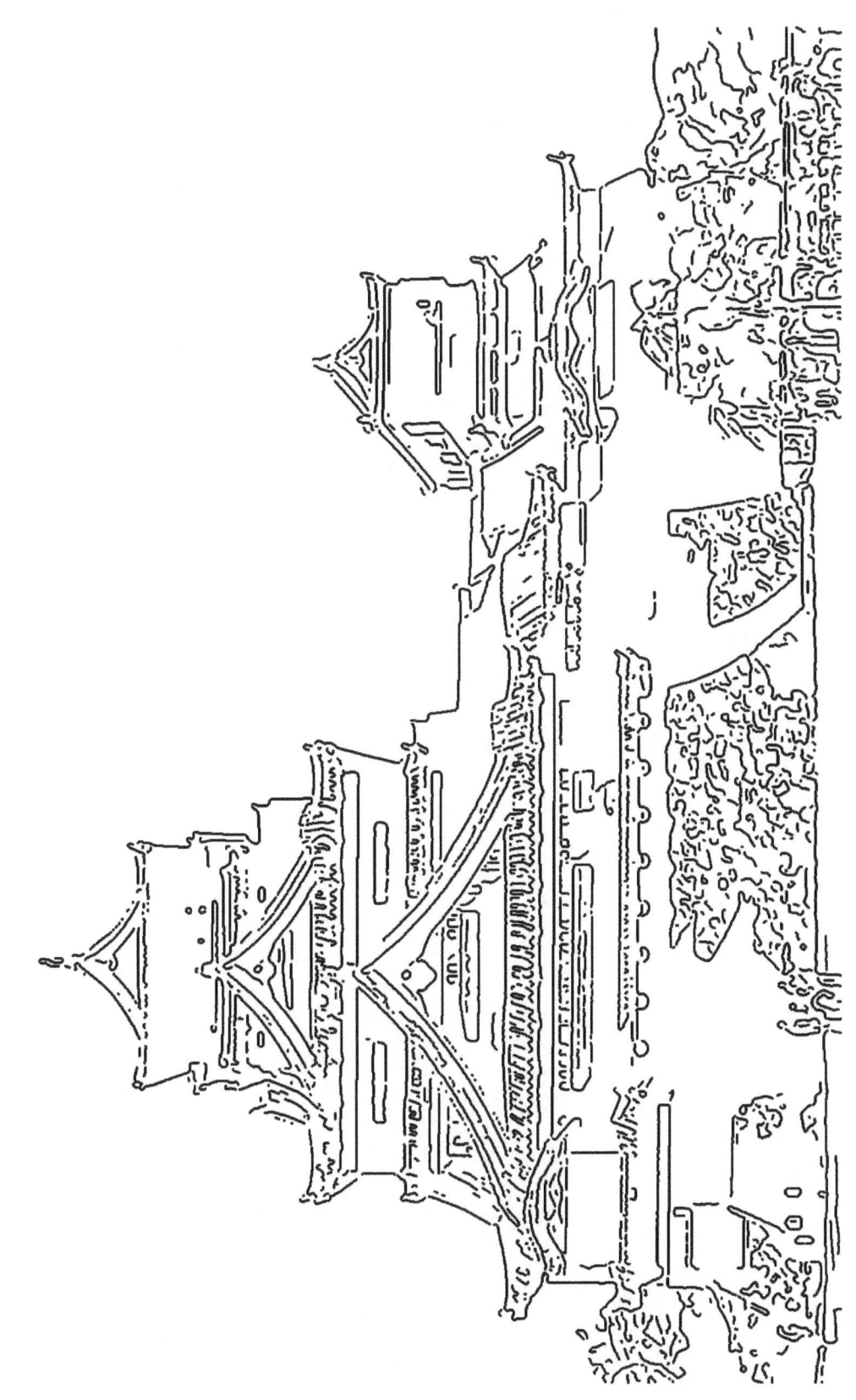

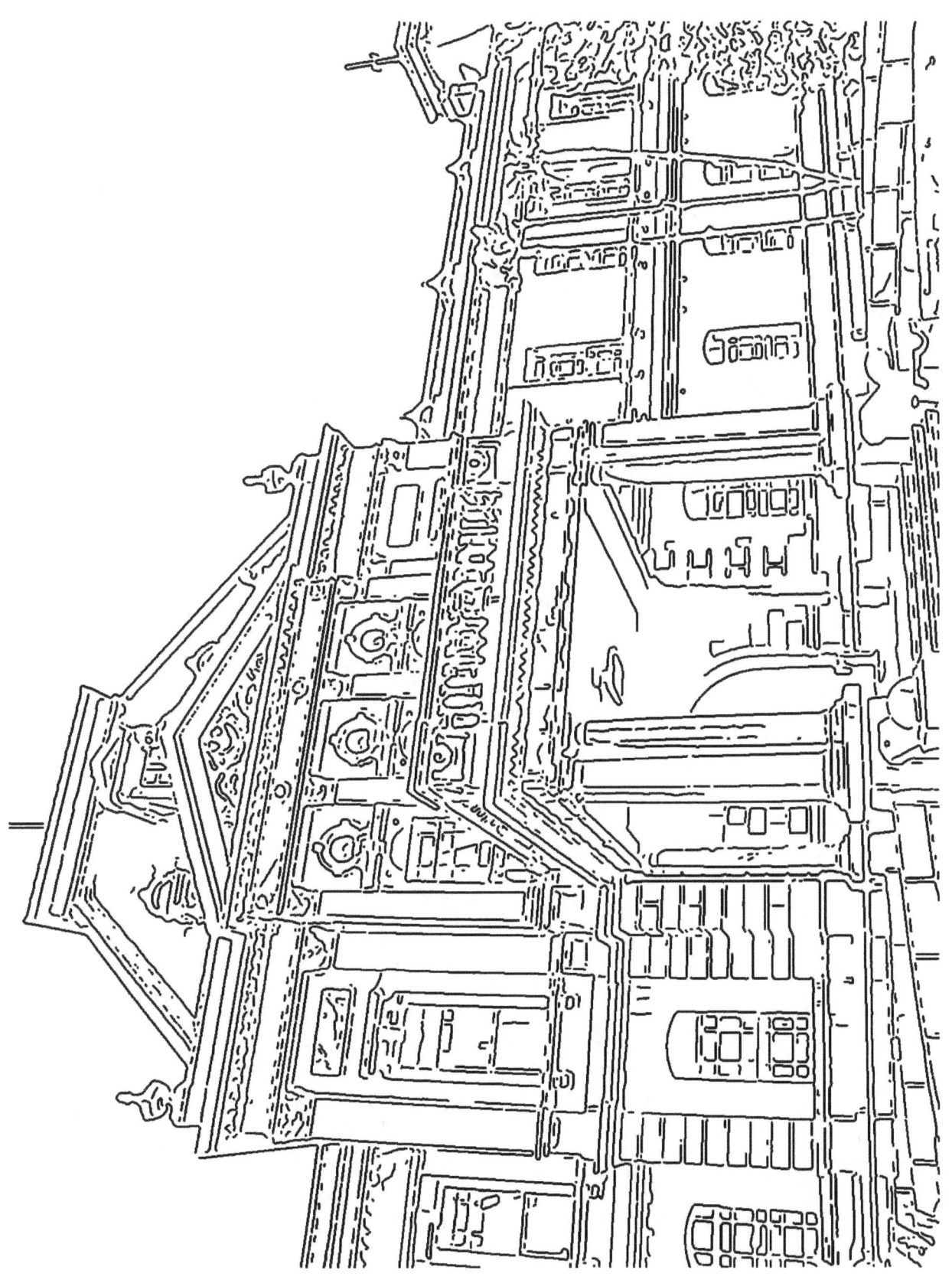

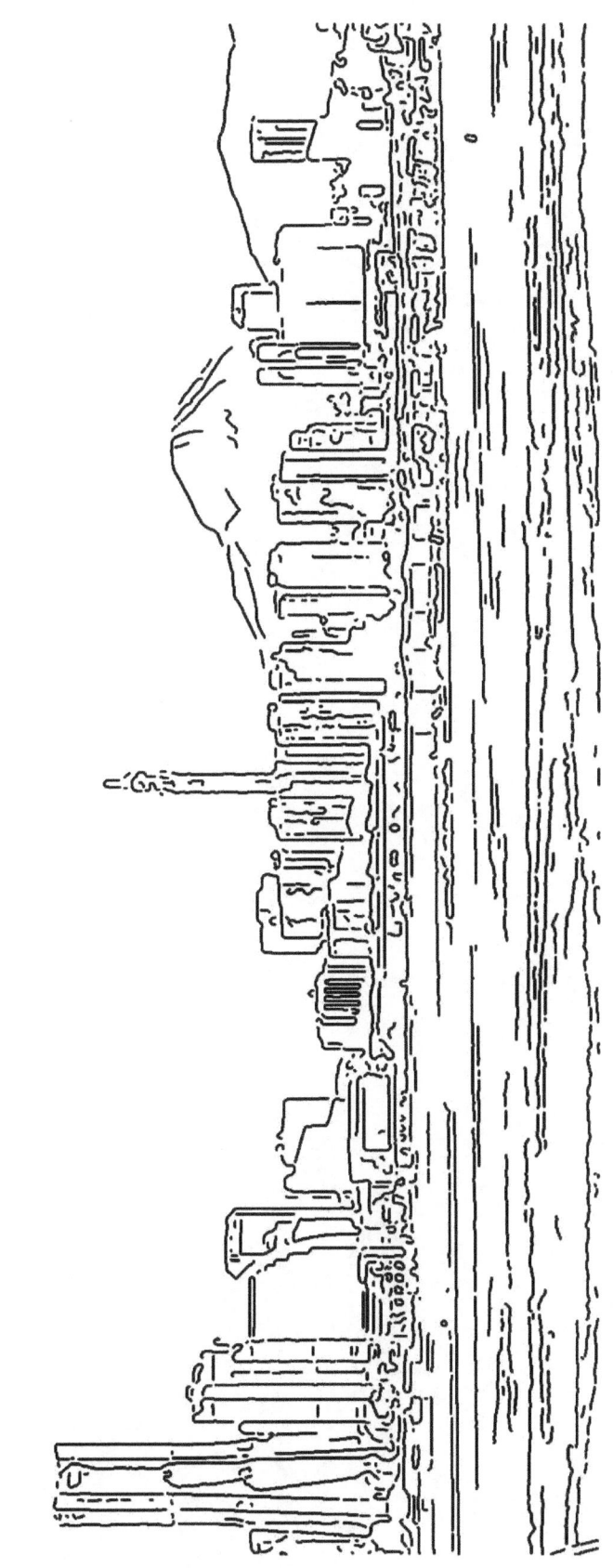

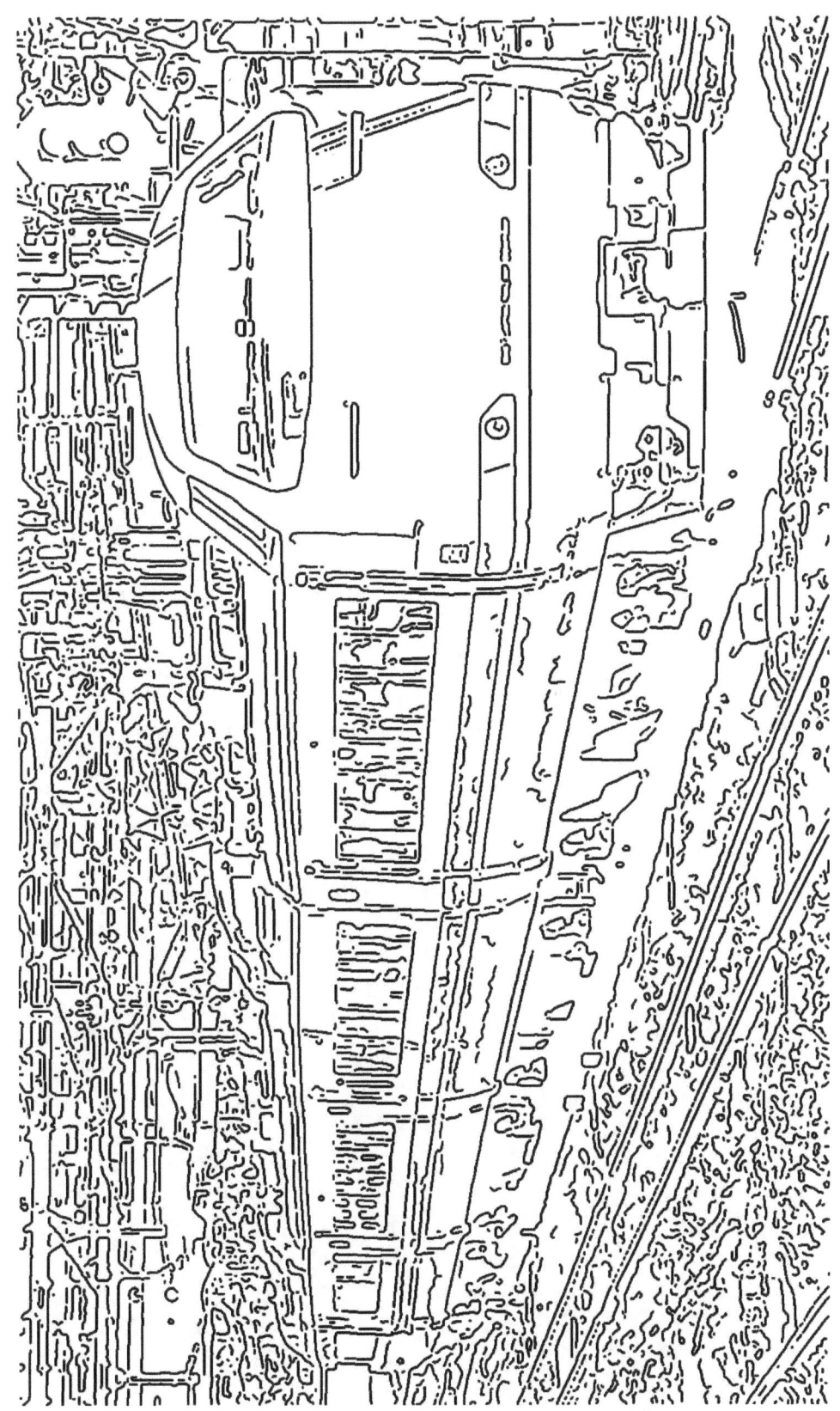

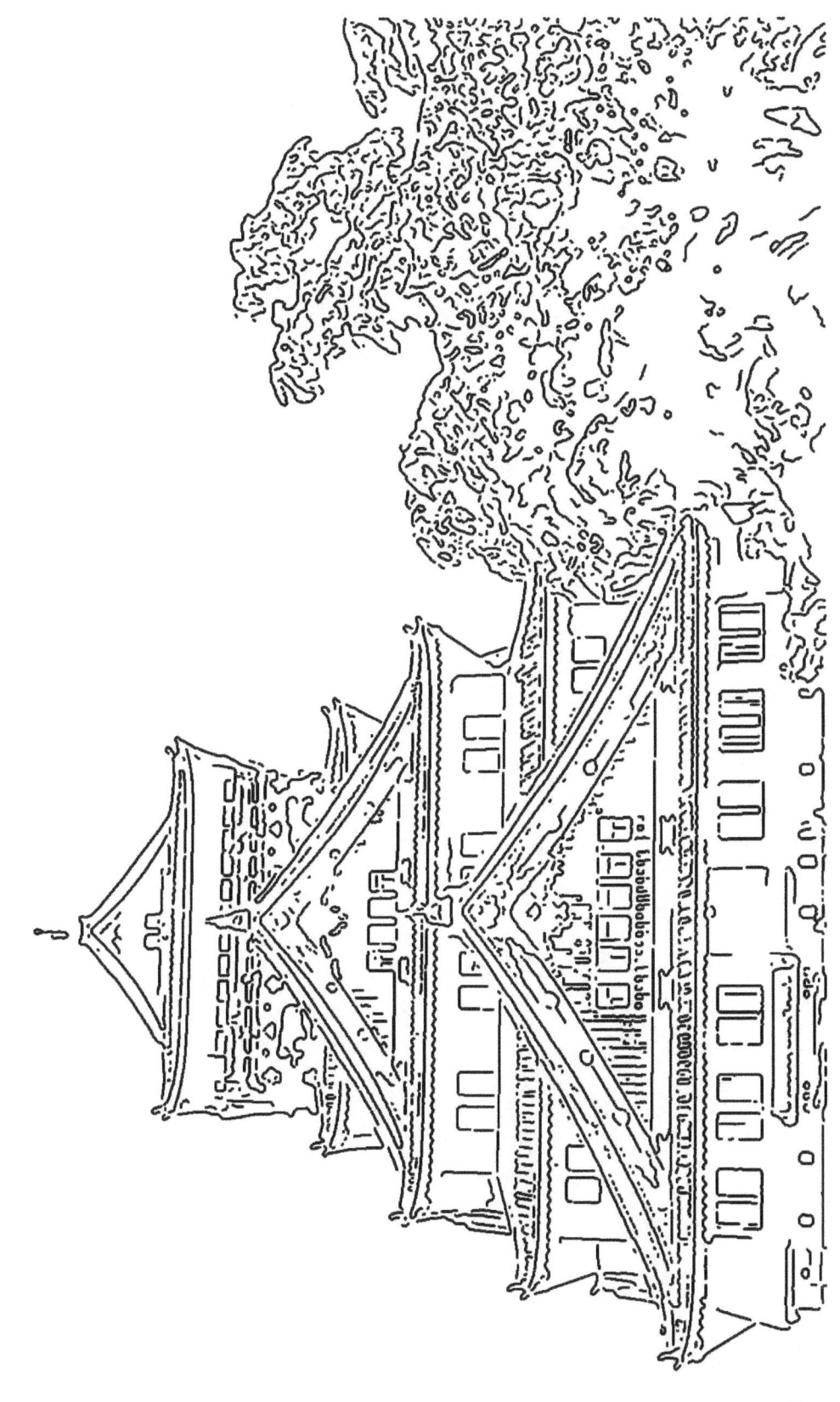

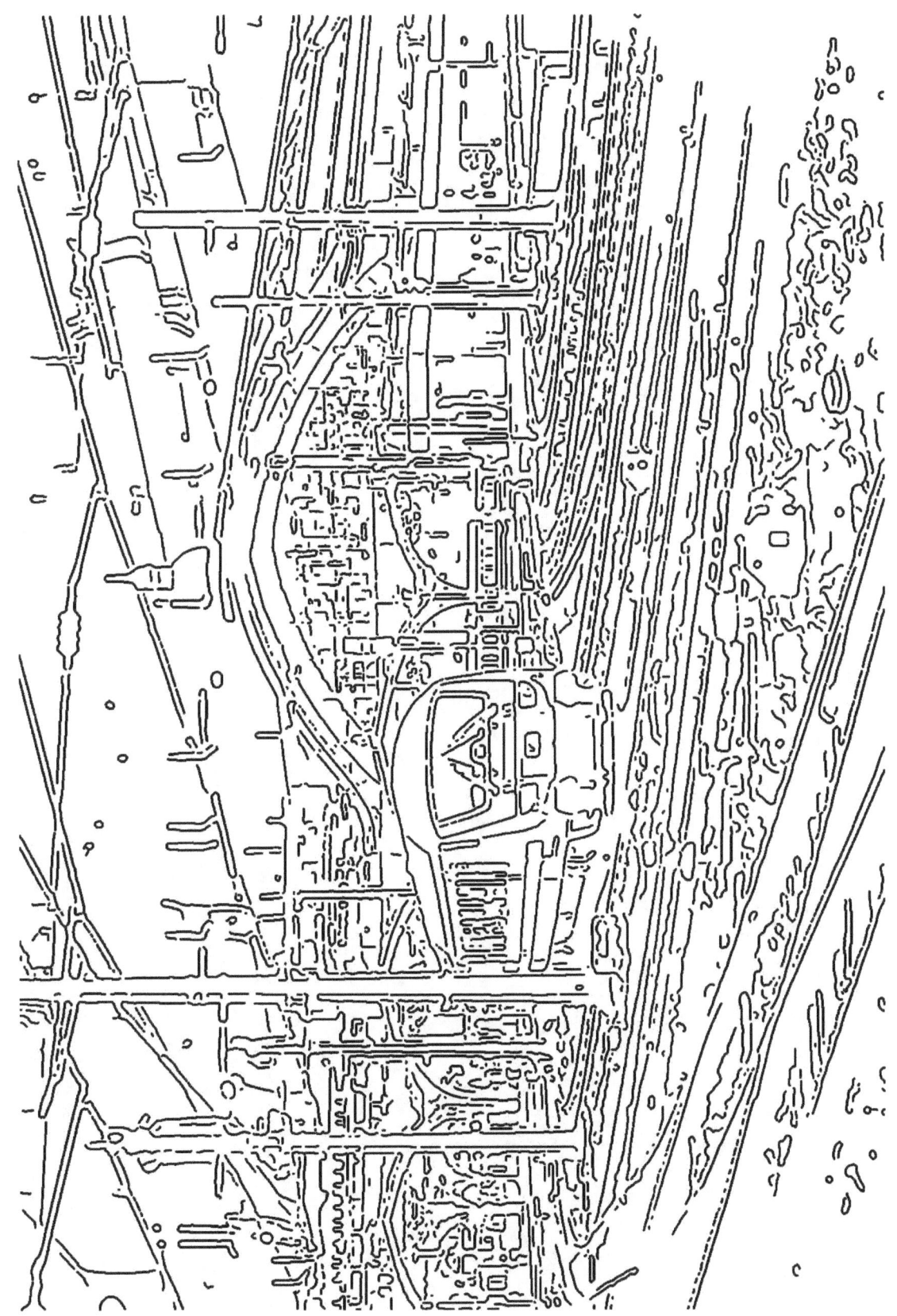

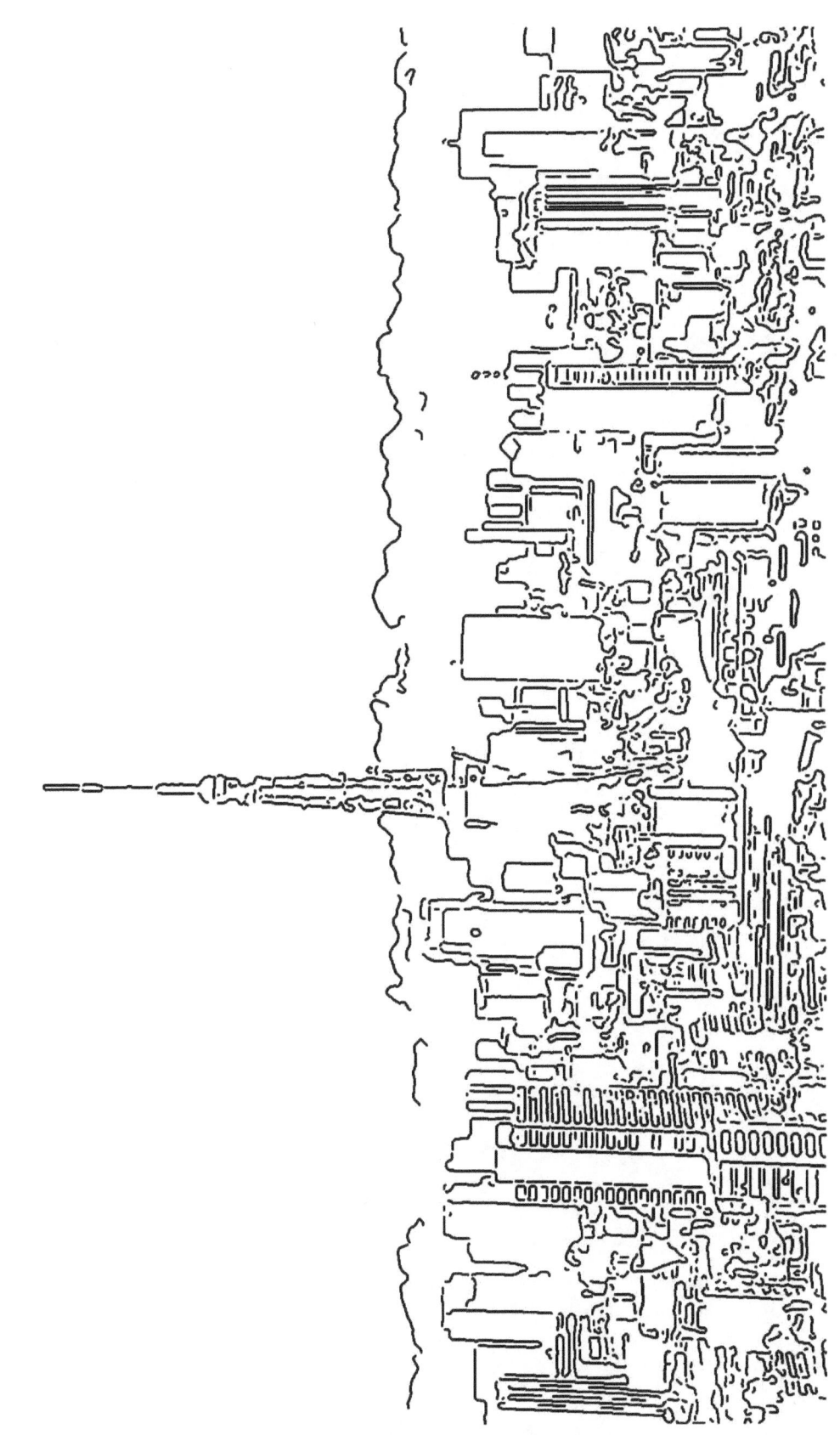

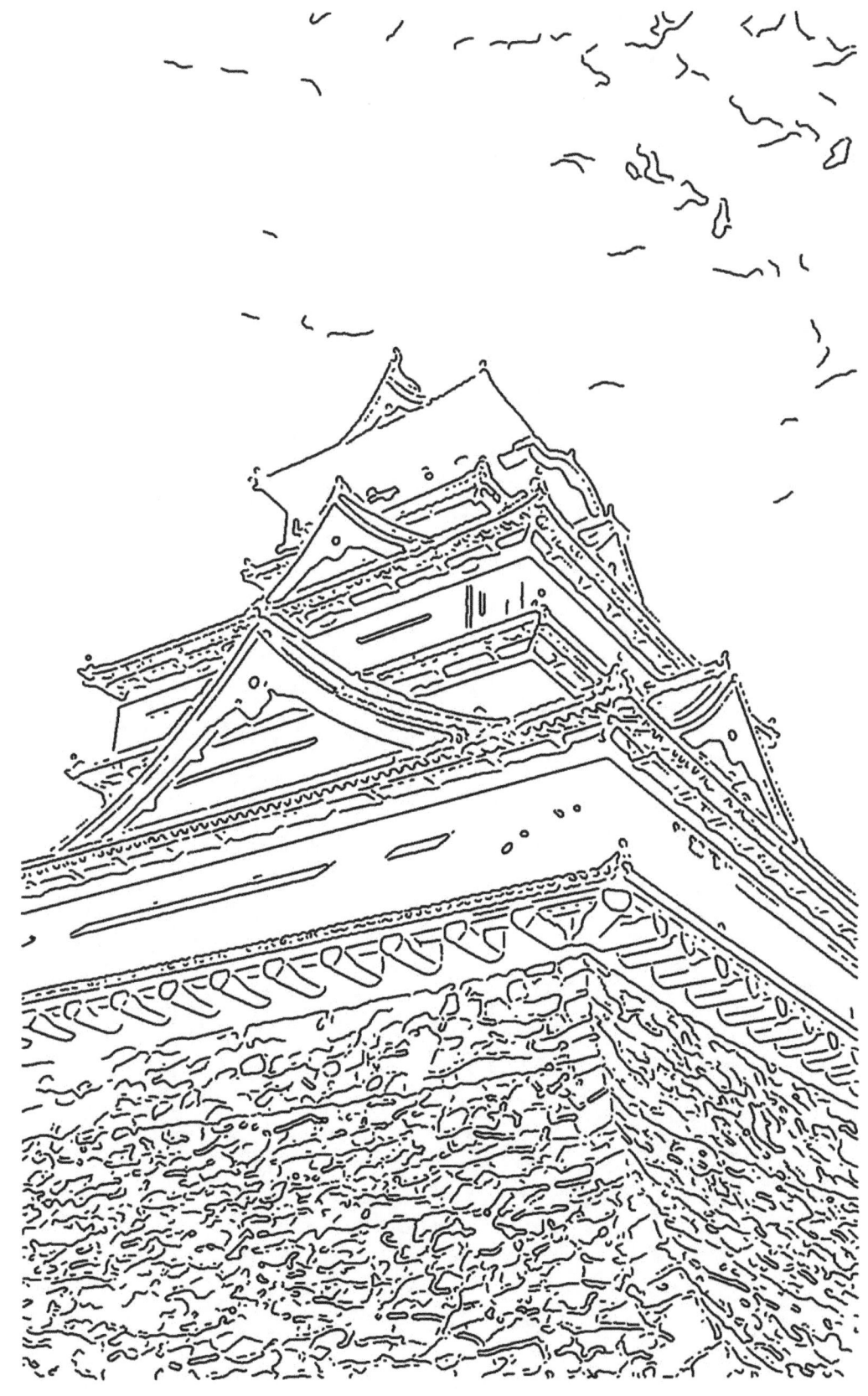

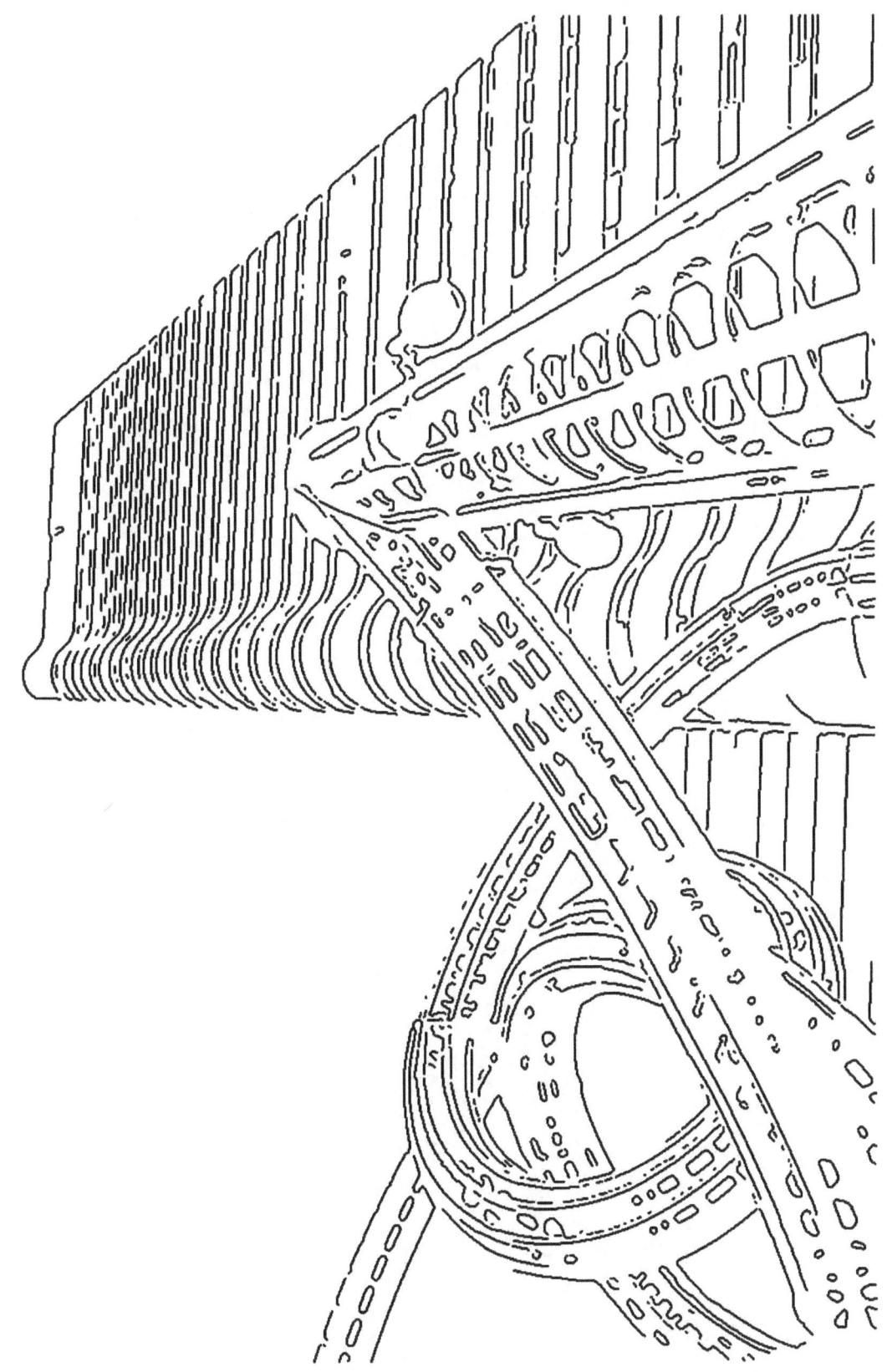

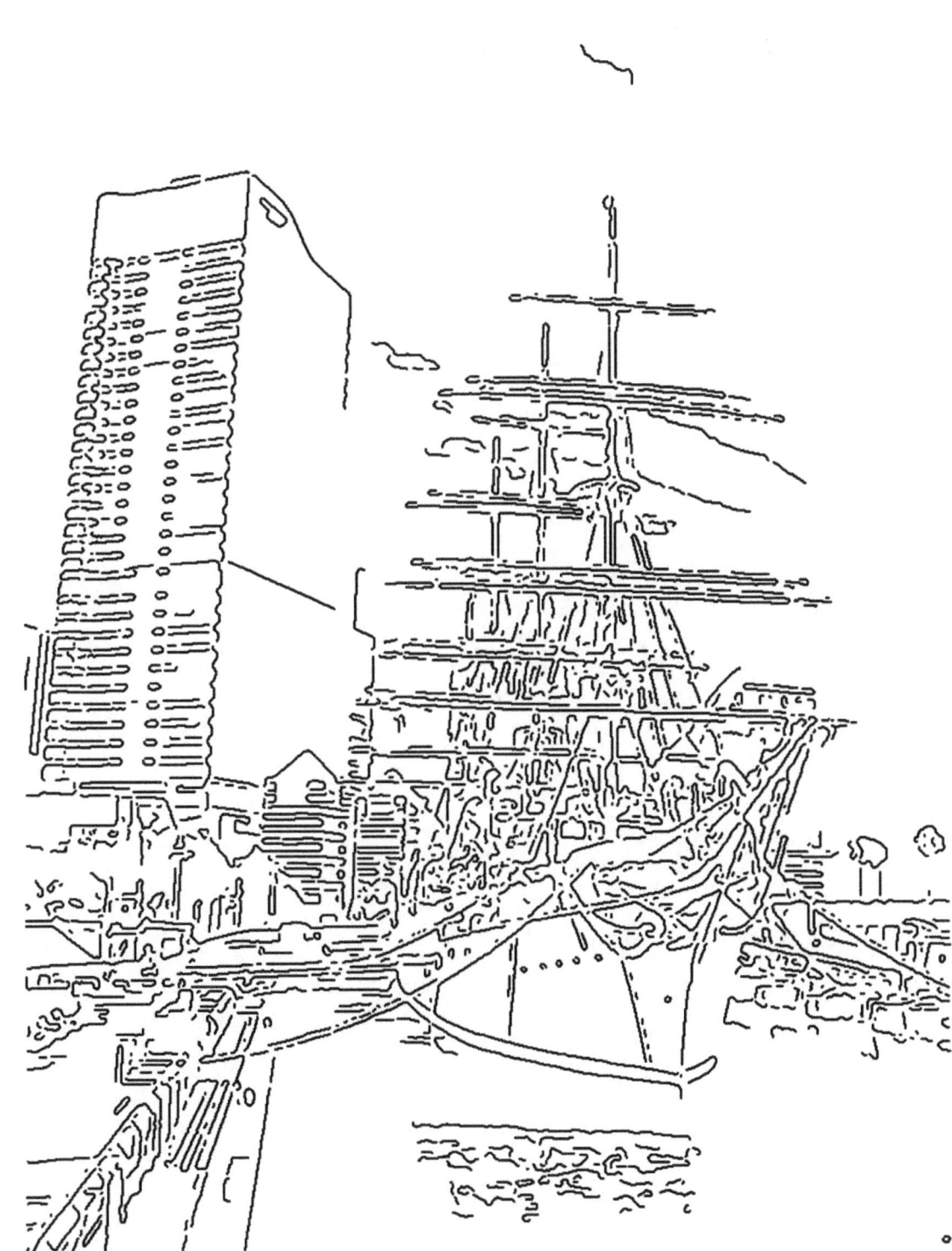

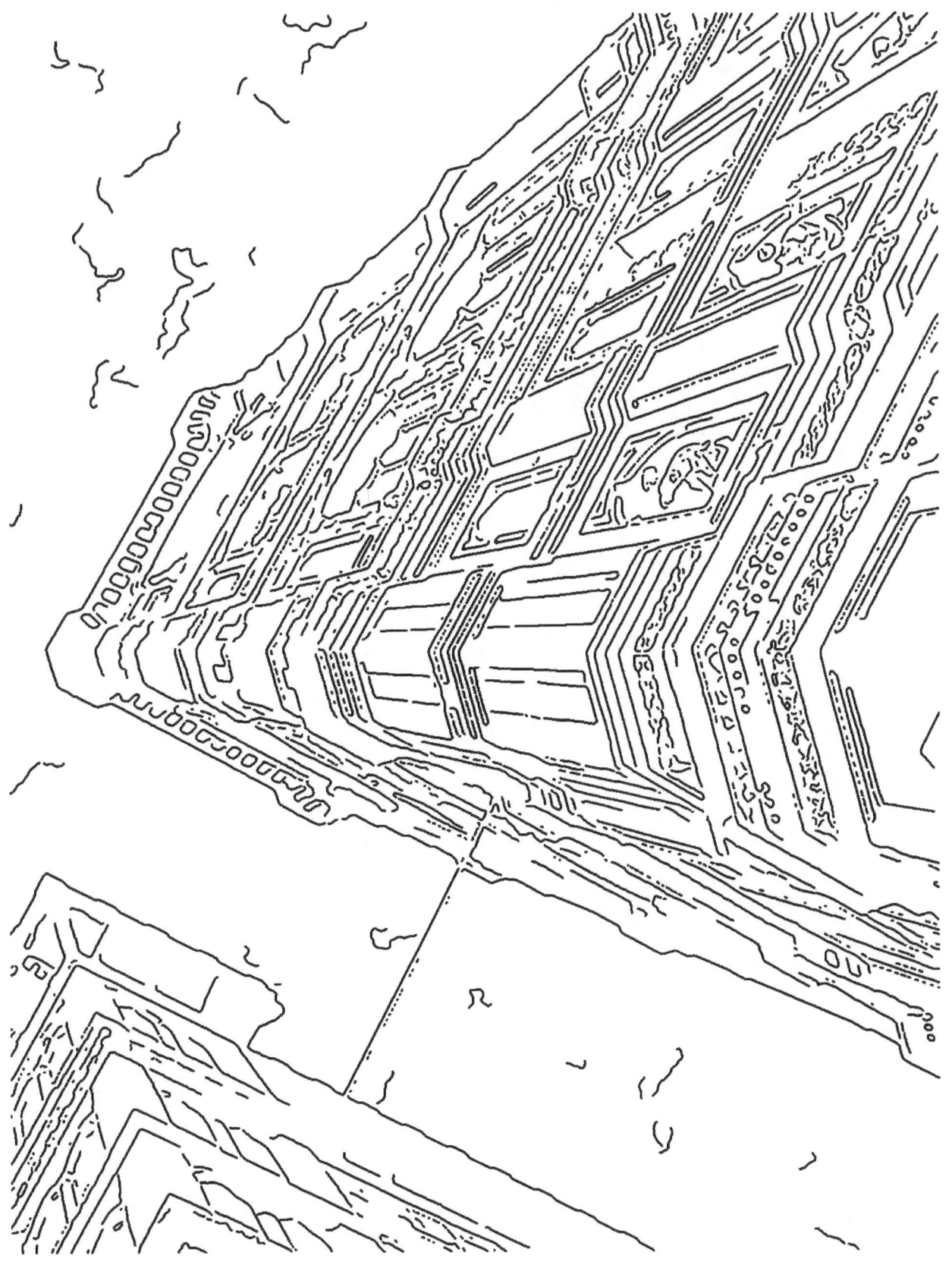

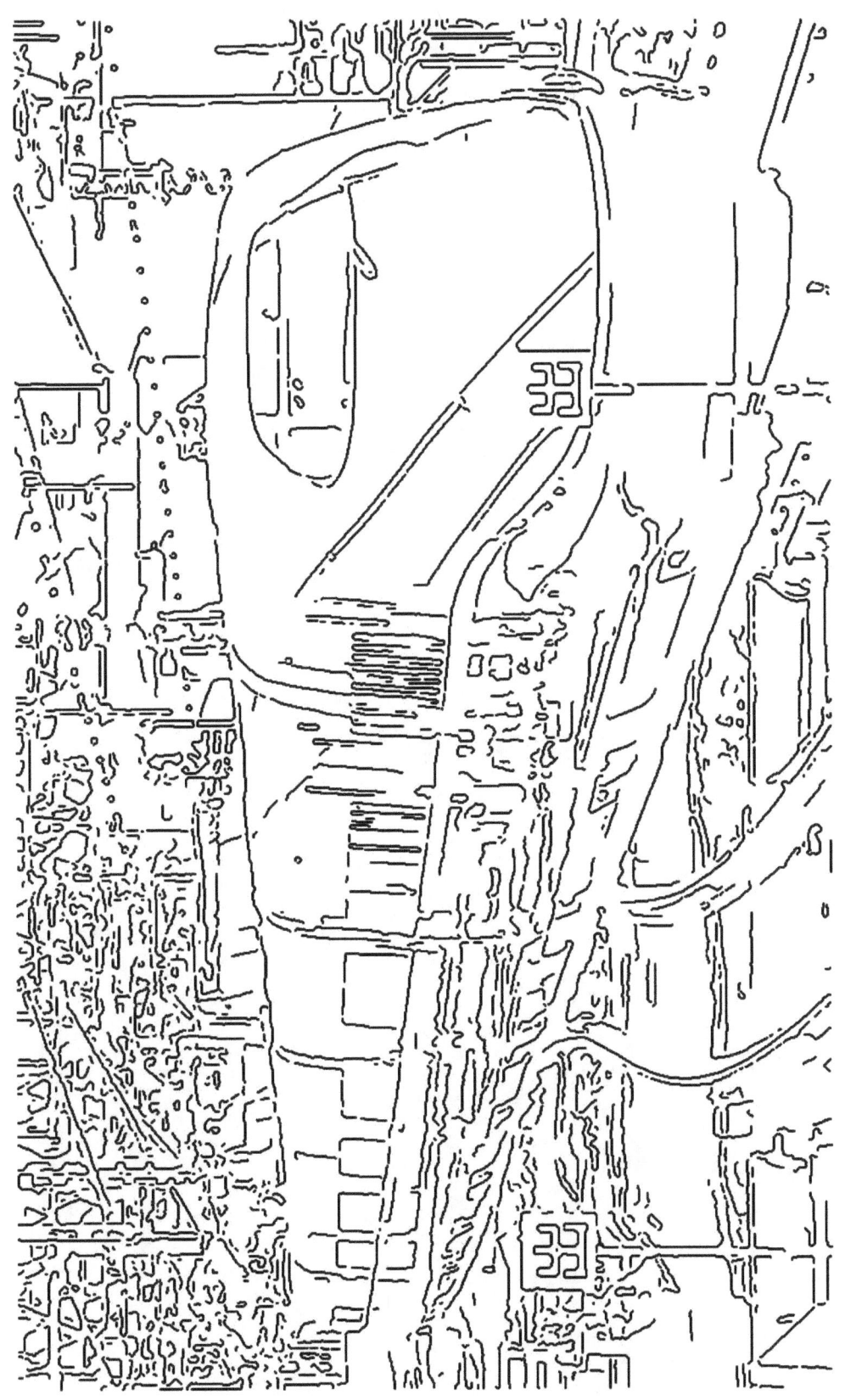

Thank you

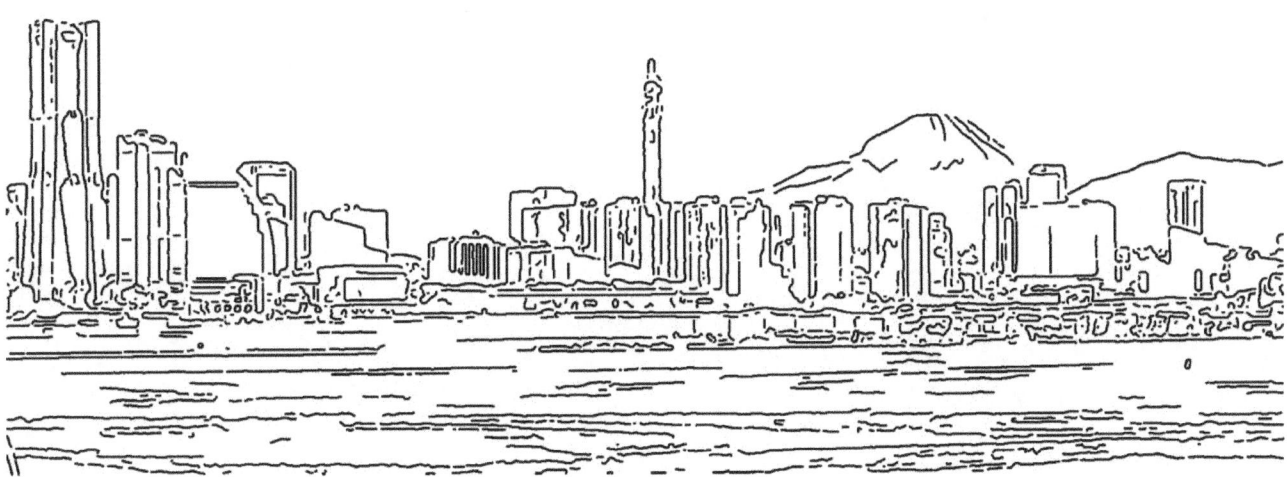

www.ingramcontent.com/pod-product-compliance
Lightning Source LLC
Chambersburg PA
CBHW080634190526
45169CB00009B/3386